Lesser Mortals

A Play

Geoff Saunders

A SAMUEL FRENCH ACTING EDITION

SAMUELFRENCH-LONDON.CO.UK
SAMUELFRENCH.COM

FOR AMATEUR PRODUCTION ENQUIRIES

UNITED KINGDOM AND WORLD
EXCLUDING NORTH AMERICA
plays@SamuelFrench-London.co.uk
020 7255 4302/01

Each title is subject to availability from Samuel French,

depending upon country of performance.

LESSER MORTALS

First presented by Drip Action Theatre in St Mary's Hall, Arundel, as part of the Arundel Festival Theatre Trail on 18th August 2012, with the following cast:

Victoria	Kathy Haigh
Wendy	Gill Medway
Tilly	Justine Richardson
Gladys	Brenda Hargraves

Director   Lin Jones

CHARACTERS

Victoria, 55
Wendy, 53
Tilly, 43
Gladys, 82

The Scene

A Quaker Meeting

LESSER MORTALS

A Quaker Meeting

At least four chairs are arranged in an arc. Wendy, Victoria and Gladys sit on three of them; the other is unoccupied. There may, if you wish, be more people onstage, sitting silently, eyes open or closed, in an arc as at a Quaker Meeting

Wendy is 53, Victoria 55 and Gladys 82. When the play opens, Gladys is asleep; Wendy and Victoria are lost in their thoughts

There is silence for a while

Victoria She was only being nice — Quakerly, I suppose — but I do wish she hadn't bothered. All I wanted this morning was an hour of peace and quiet, nobody bothering me with talk or sympathy or ... anything. But there she was, looming at me in that way she has. And I was thinking 'Don't speak to me, don't speak to me, don't speak to me' and trying to look invisible, but that didn't put her off. Loom, loom, loom she goes and then there's a silence and then:

Wendy Sarah and I would love you to join us for lunch after Meeting.

Victoria I do hope I wasn't rude. I've accepted, but I don't think my voice or my body language backed up my words ... I don't want to have lunch with them, I really don't, but ——

Wendy No idea why I said that. Never have people over for lunch. Seemed the Quakerly thing to do, though. Only been widowed two months, poor girl. Thought maybe it would cheer her up a bit. (*Pause*) Oh, goodness. Lunch is yesterday's leftover pie and yesterday's leftover mash. Fine for Sarah and me, obviously, but can't give that to Victoria. Not on its own. Oh, Wendy, stupid girl, why did you have to be kind and sociable all out of the blue? (*Pause*) Broccoli. Grab some on the way home. Covers a multitude of sins, broccoli.

Victoria Let's be positive about this. Maybe some company is just what I need. All I've wanted so far is to be left well alone. Alone doing nothing, just staring as the room gets darker around me and I realize I haven't eaten anything, done anything, even got dressed ... Then raging. Raging silently, sometimes; sometimes screaming and thumping the cushions, raging at you and your cruelty and your endless silence.

Wendy Serve what's left of the pie in the kitchen and carry it through. Cut it into four; that way Victoria can have seconds and think it's a new pie. Lots of gravy. Pie, mash, gravy, broccoli. It'll have to do.

Victoria People are trying to be kind, I know, and I should forgive them on the spot, but I hate it —I really hate it — when they say you've "taken" Ray. You don't exist, do you, you didn't "take" him anywhere. He just went. If you existed, and you wanted to "take" him — whatever that is supposed to mean — if you wanted to take him wouldn't you just, I don't know, snuff him out? He breathes in, he breathes out, he's dead, calm and painless. Why, if you are this merciful and loving all-powerful being, did you throw him off a ladder and slowly leach the life out of his broken body over the next two weeks? Answer me that? Of course you can't. Even if you existed I'm not sure you could.

Wendy Plan B. Send Sarah ahead after Meeting. Doesn't like the coffee and chat thing, anyway. Likes to maintain her inner calm. (*She looks out, "seeing" Sarah across the Meeting*) Look at her now with her mouth open, doing her Buddhist hands thing. That's yoga teaching for you. (*Pause*) Yes, send her ahead for the broccoli. That way Victoria will think we had it in already. (*Pause*) And she'd better hide some of the photos in the living-room. And some of the books. Don't want Victoria finding out we're not widowed sisters after all.

Victoria The irony, of course, is that Ray believed in you. He had — what did he call it? — a "constant relationship" with you. He used to say you were in every action he performed. He'd open the curtains and feel you there in the new day. If it was a happy day, you'd be present in the joy he was feeling, in the sunshine, in the promise of good things; if it was a bad day, you'd be there in the strength he'd need to get through it. It all came from you, it all went back to you. He said that you were in me too — that I was a gift from you, a gift that gave him happiness and grounded him in the world. I wanted so much to feel like he did. He was always so settled and calm, even when everything seemed to be going wrong, even when he was lying in that hospital bed, every breath a huge effort. I used to think if I could be like him I'd be so much happier. I believed in his belief; I could see it working. But why couldn't I — why can't I — believe? Why can't I have a "constant relationship"? If you existed, you'd have been there for me, wouldn't you? Then I'd have believed.

Wendy On the other hand ... On the other hand, maybe this is our chance to come out. Been coming to this Meeting for years and always maintained this lie that we're sisters. What the hell for? Quakers are the most accepting people going. Accept people whatever their creed or beliefs or habits — or try to, anyway. Don't always entirely succeed; only human, after all. (*Pause*) Not sure why we lied to them in the first place. Scared, perhaps, despite the tolerance. And of course honesty is a big thing with Quakers so it's hard to turn round now and confess to telling porkies. And of course if we tell them we've been lying they might well be offended that we felt we needed to ...

Tilly enters. She is 43, well-dressed and attractive. She wears slightly too much make-up. She sits in the available chair

Tilly Sorry I'm late! It's only been twenty years! That's when you last saw me — or saw me in a Quaker Meeting, anyway! Twenty years ago! But I'm back! And, yes, you've got it, I'm wearing make-up! Not very Quakerly, am I? But this isn't make-up, no, it isn't, not really — it's liberation!

Victoria Before you ask, yes, Ray's relationship with you annoyed me. I was jealous of you. You got to hear his thoughts, you got to share his worries. He could have — he should have — shared them with me. But thanks to you he didn't need to. I felt shut out. And I envied him as well. Clocking up the Deadly Sins, aren't I?

Tilly Of course you know all this — it's me that's been away, not you — but I just want to say it anyway. OK, confession time — I'm glad that Ken is dead. Actually glad. Sorry, sorry, that's definitely not a Quakerly thing to say, but it's the truth. And being truthful is Quakerly, isn't it? Tell you something, I'm hooked on the truth at the moment! I've lived with lies so long I get a rush when I tell the truth! (*Pause*) Well, anyway ... Ken was fine before we married and for a few months after, and then I realized — with such a shock — that I'd married someone who didn't want to be my husband, he wanted to be my father — and a bossy, angry, controlling father at that. I knew things had changed when I was just about to leave the house to go shopping and he said "You're not going out in that". Not those words exactly, but close. I can't remember what I was wearing but it can't have been that outrageous; I've never had the legs for outrageous. I just froze. It was a father's tone of voice — but not a tone my own father'd ever used. I nearly laughed but I knew by then when Ken was joking and when he wasn't. And that was it. No more nice clothes.

Victoria Ray was a marvel, really. He managed to be calm and wise and balanced — without fail — but was never remotely patronizing. If he'd been pompous or snooty or looked down his nose at us lesser mortals, just once, I could have coped better. It would have reduced him ever so slightly to my level. But thanks to you, it was impossible to dislike him, impossible to resent him or get angry with him ... Can you imagine how bloody irritating that was?

Tilly Ken was clever. He used my Quaker beliefs against me. He wasn't a Quaker, no way, but he loved flinging his version of Quaker ideas around. "You're supposed to be plain and modest," he said to me, "so be a good Quaker and stop dressing like a tart." "I don't dress like a tart," I said. "You bloody do," he came back with. "You want all the blokes eyeing you up, don't you?" "No I don't," I said. "I dress to look good for you — and for myself." "Is that Quakerly? Is that modest and moral?" he asked. He was smiling a sideways smile like some sort of hyena. "I'm not just a Quaker, I'm a woman as well," I told him, "and women are allowed to look good." (*Pause*) And he exploded. I've never been so frightened in my life. And of course I had to dress modestly for the next couple of weeks — long sleeves, high neck — so no-one would see the bruises.

Wendy Be funny if Adam turned up here now, wouldn't it? For one thing, he's supposed to have died in 1982! For another, his ex-wife now lives with another woman and is blissfully happy. And has three cats. Oh, dear, three cats — such a cliché, I know, but we're comfortable with that.

Tilly I was the clichéd abused wife from then on. For nearly twenty-three years. (*Pause*) To start with, I was a bit rebellious, remember? He decided I shouldn't attend Meeting any more because it "gave me ideas" so I tried to sneak out one Sunday morning — and got caught by the back door. "I'm just going to the shops for a few things," I said. He did the hyena smile. "I'll give you a lift then", he said. And drove me into town, past the Meeting House, and all the time I was desperately thinking of what I could buy that we didn't already have at home ... Tinned peas and custard powder, I seem to remember ... (*Pause*) He knew. He knew exactly what I'd been up to. So, from then on, he'd find us little projects to do on a Sunday morning so he could keep an eye on me. And, as soon as he could, he moved us down here, miles away. (*Pause*) Here's the stupid thing. The stupid thing is that after a while I thought he was right. I was a tart, so I reformed myself; I threw all my makeup away and wore really dowdy, unflattering clothes. I cut my hair with the kitchen scissors and didn't care if people stared at me. I was stupid — he told me — so I didn't pick up a book for years. I was bad with money — he told me — so I was glad he gave me a shopping allowance every week and nothing else. And of course I would be a lousy mother so we never had kids. Know something? I somehow persuaded myself he was controlling everything because he loved me. Because I was a lost cause and he was being generous and kind and taking care of me. He could do the job of caring for me so much better than the Quakers, or my doctor, or my friends ... And the bruises just showed how unworthy I was of his love and care, how disappointed he was in me ... They showed I couldn't behave myself properly ...

Victoria I used to wait for you to appear to me. I've given up now. I used to sit in Meeting willing you to appear, longing for a flash of light, a warm glow all around me, maybe even a voice or a vision. But nothing. You'd appeared to Ray. He could see you, feel you, drink you in a cup of tea. So I thought, well, I'm next. You'll reveal yourself in all your glory and make me feel complete and serene, like Ray. But you haven't. And why not? Because you can't. Because you'd have to be here to do that, wouldn't you?

Wendy Don't imagine Victoria's anti-gay. Done the Greenham thing, done the Women's Group thing, must have seen all sides. Hardly know her, that's the trouble. Always kept themselves to themselves, Ray and Victoria. She's been even quieter since he died. (*Pause*) We'll tell her but ask her not to tell anyone else. That's the best way. (*Pause*) She'll know the moment she steps in the door. Lack of a second bedroom, that's a dead giveaway. Shame there's no downstairs loo; she'll have to go upstairs. One peek in the study and she'll know. (*Pause*) Bloody ridiculous! It's the twenty-first century! Why am I so worried about this? (*Pause*) Send Sarah ahead to pick up the broccoli, hide the photos and books, set the Z-bed up in the study in case Victoria gets a bit nosy ...

There follows a pause. The women all sit in silence, thinking or not thinking or, in Gladys's case, sleeping. This pause depicts what a Quaker Meeting looks like from outside the minds of its participants. It can last as long as you like, but at least two minutes would be good

Gladys wakes with a start!

Gladys Heavens! Oh! (*She looks around*) Oh, I'm here. I'm
here. I thought I was at home. I thought Alfie was with me. I
must have been dreaming ...

I like dreaming about Alfie. I didn't used to. But it's been a
while now, so to see him smiling at me, maybe walking along
the canal with his stick hooked over his arm ... I like it.

It's a gift from you, isn't it? Seeing Alfie again in my dreams.

What I saw just now was Alfie when I first met him. 1948 in
the Brighton Meeting House. Gazing at me across the Meeting.
And there I was in my dream, gazing back, just as I did then.

Back in '48 I thought: not very Quakerly behaviour, Gladys;
we're supposed to be communing, waiting for you, and here I
am just staring and staring at this beautiful man, bold as brass.

He was beautiful. So upright and dapper and well-groomed.
Vain, a bit, but I liked that. He took care of himself and had
some pride.

I knew all about the drinking from the word go. He had a little
flask in his pocket — very elegant it was, these days one would
say "sexy" — and it had brandy in it and he poured some in
his tea after Meeting.

Bold as brass!

It didn't put me off him at all. There I was, teetotal like a good
Quaker girl, and I should have been shocked and repulsed. But
no, it was sexy. He was beautiful and he was ... just a little bit
dangerous. Delicious.

Of course the flask was just the tip of the iceberg. He couldn't
get through an hour without a drink. Brandy. Whisky. Gin.
Never beer; "it's just not strong enough," he'd say. And by the
end of the day he'd be in a dreadful state. Every single day.

At the beginning, everyone said: "Don't get involved with him". No-one understood. No-one understood that from the moment I met him — there in the tearoom at Meeting, watching him lace his tea with brandy — I just loved him. I loved his pride and his vanity and his danger, and I loved his brokenness and his sadness. All I wanted to do was be with him and care for him and love him.

I knew I'd never leave him.

He tried to leave me. He'd disappear for days on end and when I'd track him down he'd look at me with such remorse it would break my heart. Shame, that's what it was, and beneath that the hope that one day I wouldn't come and he'd find oblivion.

Remember Hastings? 1957, I think it was ... Standing on that railway platform, crying, crying, his suit ruined, his trilby smashed, just saying over and over "Don't take me back, Gladys, leave me here to die, it's what I deserve", and people looking, and me, ramrod-straight, defying their stares, somehow proud of my husband despite ... despite everything.

Was Alfie a test? Did you take a look at my comfortable child-hood and my perfect teenage years and my healthy family with their strong convictions and tender wisdom and think: right, let's test her mettle? Did you? Did you think, "Let's give her love, romance, a helpmeet, a companion — but make him a broken, troubled, unhappy man in need of a more complicated kind of love"? Is that what you thought?

Because if it was ... Thank you.

Of course you were testing him, too. Sometimes he thought he'd won. He used to tick off days on the calendar when he'd managed not to have a drink — do you remember? — and if he fell, he'd start again. One day he got to forty days, the longest he'd ever managed. He cried. I cried for him. He was the happiest I'd ever seen him. But of course he was so happy he had to have a drink to celebrate.

When he was sober he was the sweetest man alive. When he was drunk ... Well, he wasn't sweet, was he? He was frightened and unhappy. The worse he got, the more determined I was to help him. Love against the odds — that's true love, I always think. And that's what we had, Alfie and me.

I'll always be grateful to you for that. You made me work hard for my happiness but that just made it all the sweeter.

Perhaps a few years more with Alfie would have been nice. You did take him ever so young, really. But I'm not complaining. He made me happy and I know I made him happy. Can't ask for more, can I ...?

Gladys drifts back off to sleep

Wendy Sort of test, isn't it? I have a Quakerly moment and open my big mouth and invite Victoria round for lunch, but what's really happening is I'm gearing up to come out to the Meeting. That's what Sarah would say. She'd say we never do anything by chance. Always a reason behind everything. Take ourselves by surprise to make ourselves move on. (*Pause*) Perhaps I should just stand up and minister. Tell all. Tell everyone about living with lies and covering things up and worrying what others will think. Yes. Now!

Tilly Twenty years! Twenty years since I last set foot in a Quaker Meeting! And I feel at home already. Not one of them has spoken to me — apart from the lady at the door — and yet I know already I'm amongst friends. I wonder what they think of me — all this make-up, glammed up to the nines? I wonder what they'd think if they knew that I'm smiling this big smile because my horrible husband is dead. (*Pause*) I guess they'd try to understand, I suppose ...

Wendy Would they understand? Understand why I've lied to
them for so long. Why we've lied to them for so long. Would
they forgive us? Of course they would ...

*There is a silence. Not as long as the previous one, but long enough for
everyone to settle ...*

Victoria I love it when no-one speaks, when we all sit in glorious
silence for an hour. The peace. My thoughts can go where they
want, or they can go nowhere. I can stare at the trees outside
and drift away ... Lovely.
Wendy Right! That's it! I'm going to tell them. Sarah would want
me to do this! Let's be honest about ourselves and if anyone
disapproves — that's their problem! (*She stands*)
Victoria I made that happen. Typical.
Wendy Oh no! Done it! Committed myself and stood up! Got
to say something now!
Victoria It's always Wendy. She can't resist, can she? I bet it's
something about her cat ...
Wendy (*out loud*) Friends ... (*To herself*) No! Sarah's glaring at
me! What a face!
Victoria Do get on with it ...
Wendy It's as if she knows ... And that's definitely a "say nothing
about it" face she's making ...
Tilly Oh dear, that poor woman's completely dried ...
Wendy Can't tell them now, can I? Not with Sarah looking like
that. "Don't you dare!" her face is saying. How did she know ...?
Victoria Poor Wendy ... Just sit yourself down, love, nobody
minds ...
Wendy (*out loud*) Friends ...
Victoria Here we go. (*Looking upwards*) Sorry.
Wendy (*out loud*) I was looking at my cat Ruffle this morning ...
Victoria Of course you were! (*Looking upwards*) Sorry again.
Wendy (*out loud*) And Ruffle is so perfect it made me think
of the perfection of creation we see around us every day and
take for granted. I'm so happy to live in this beautiful world.

Tilly Sweet.

Wendy (*to herself*) Oh, goodness, that was awful. What will Victoria think of me now ...? And Sarah's still giving me the oddest look. Relief, partly, I think, so that's good ... Sit down, Wendy. (*She sits*)

Silence

Gladys slowly wakes up during the following

Tilly I won't always be like this; promise! I'll do the Quaker thing soon and see things from Ken's point of view as well as my own. But I've spent years not having my own point of view, so now I'm making up for lost time. (*Pause*) And he even took you away. That's the kind of husband he was. So it's nice to be back with you after all these years.

Victoria Would I feel any better if I thought someone was listening? Probably not. I come here week after week, I rage and seethe and want to throw things, and I never feel any better. Worse, sometimes. And you don't help, which is fair enough, I guess, as you don't exist. But answer me this: you don't exist, so why can't I stop talking to you?

Wendy We'll talk about it, Sarah and I ... Maybe soon we can let people know what's what. I'd like that. You probably would, too, wouldn't you? You love us like anyone else.

Gladys Oh, dear, I wish I could stay awake for a whole Meeting. But then, I'm old, I need to sleep ...

I like the idea of you watching over me, awake or asleep. You've always been at my side and you always will be. I'm not sure how I know that, but I do.

There is a silence. Wendy glances at her watch. A pause. Then Wendy shakes hands with whoever is nearest and they all shake hands with each other, smiling, saying hello, coming back from their thoughts into the outside world ... The traditional end to a Quaker Meeting

Wendy (*out loud*) Good morning, Friends! Let's get some tea and then Sarah can do the notices!

Black-out (or they all head off towards the tea room)

FURNITURE AND PROPERTY LIST

On stage: 4 chairs (minimum)

www.ingramcontent.com/pod-product-compliance
Ingram Content Group UK Ltd.
Pitfield, Milton Keynes, MK11 3LW, UK
UKHW021818150726
7214IPUK00017B/187